What Every Teacher Should Know About

Learning, Memory, and the Brain

What Every Teacher Should Know About...

What Every Teacher Should Know About
Diverse Learners

What Every Teacher Should Know About
Student Motivation

What Every Teacher Should Know About
Learning, Memory, and the Brain

What Every Teacher Should Know About
Instructional Planning

What Every Teacher Should Know About
Effective Teaching Strategies

What Every Teacher Should Know About
Classroom Management and Discipline

What Every Teacher Should Know About
Student Assessment

What Every Teacher Should Know About
Special Learners

What Every Teacher Should Know About
Media and Technology

What Every Teacher Should Know About
The Profession and Politics of Teaching

DONNA WALKER TILESTON

What Every Teacher Should Know About
Learning, Memory, and the Brain

CORWIN PRESS
A Sage Publications Company
Thousand Oaks, California

For information:

Corwin Press
A Sage Publications Company
2455 Teller Road
Thousand Oaks, California 91320
www.corwinpress.com

Sage Publications Ltd.
6 Bonhill Street
London EC2A 4PU
United Kingdom

Sage Publications India Pvt. Ltd.
B-42, Panchsheel Enclave
Post Box 4109
New Delhi 110 017 India

Printed in the United States of America

Library of Congress Cataloging-in-Publication Data

Tileston, Donna Walker.
What every teacher should know about learning, memory, and the brain / Donna Walker Tileston.
    p. cm. — (What every teacher should know about— ; 3)
Includes bibliographical references and index.
ISBN 0-7619-3119-8 (pbk.)
    1. Learning, Psychology of. 2. Cognitive learning. I. Title. II. Series.
LB1060.T55 2004
370.15′23—dc21   2003011793

This book is printed on acid-free paper.

    04   05   06   10   9   8   7   6   5   4   3

Acquisitions Editor:	Faye Zucker
Editorial Assistant:	Stacy Wagner
Production Editor:	Diane S. Foster
Copy Editor:	Kristin Bergstad
Typesetter:	C&M Digitals (P) Ltd.
Proofreader:	Mary Meagher
Indexer:	Molly Hall
Cover Designer:	Tracy E. Miller
Production Artist:	Lisa Miller

Contents

About the Author

Donna Walker Tileston, Ed.D., is a veteran teacher of 27 years and the president of Strategic Teaching and Learning, a consulting firm that provides services to schools throughout the United States and Canada. Also an author, Donna's publications include *Strategies for Teaching Differently: On the Block or Not* (Corwin Press, 1998), *Innovative Strategies of the Block Schedule* (Bureau of Education and Research [BER], 1999), and *Ten Best Teaching Practices: How Brain Research, Learning Styles, and Standards Define Teaching Competencies* (Corwin Press, 2000), which has been on Corwin's best-seller list since its first year in print.

Donna received her B.A. from the University of North Texas, her M.A. from East Texas State University, and her Ed.D. from Texas A & M University-Commerce. She may be reached at www.strategicteachinglearning.com or by e-mail at dwtileston@yahoo.com.

Acknowledgments

M y sincere thanks go to my Acquisitions Editor, Faye Zucker, for her faith in education and what this information can do to help all children be successful. Without Faye, these books would not have been possible.

I had the best team of editors around: Diane Foster, Stacy Wagner, and Stacey Shimizu. You took my words and you gave them power. Thank you.

Thanks to my wonderful Board Chairman at Strategic Teaching and Learning, Dulany Howland: Thank you for sticking with me in the good times and the tough spots. Your expertise and friendship have been invaluable.

To my wonderful son, Kevin L. McBrayer.
The world is a better place because you are a part of it.

Introduction

Learning is not just a process left to the brain, it involves the whole being. This book examines how learning occurs and the implications for helping all students to be successful. In these chapters, we will look at the factors that identify being smart and the factors that label us as slow learners or underachievers. We will examine the factors that help students take in information at a more efficient rate and the factors that help students to retrieve information from long-term memory. We will also examine the tactics that help students learn and remember declarative knowledge and the importance of procedural tools. Practical applications will help the reader to make connections between the information on how learning occurs and ways to prepare and teach effective lessons.

One of the most important things we can do for our students today is to teach them the vocabulary they will need to be successful in the lessons and assessments given. Teach vocabulary first and see what a difference it makes. In Form 0.1 are the vocabulary words needed for this book. In the "Your Definition" column, write in your understanding of the word at this time. After you have read the book, see if you have changed your mind about your definition or if you want to enhance your first thoughts about the words in the "Revised Definition" column. I am also including a vocabulary pre-test for you to assess your understanding at this time.

Form 0.1   Vocabulary List for Learning, Memory, and the Brain

Vocabulary Word	Your Definition	Your Revised Definition
Achievement gap		
Active learning		
Basic skills		
Brain-based teaching		
Coaching		
Constructivism		
Declarative knowledge		
Differentiated instruction		
Episodic memory		
Explicit instruction		
Graphic organizers		
Heuristics		
Indirect instruction		
Cognitive development		
Mastery learning		
Metacognition		
Procedural memory		
Procedural knowledge		
Pedagogy		
Semantic memory		
Scaffolding		
Teaching for understanding		

Vocabulary
Pre-Test

Instructions: For each question, choose the one best answer.

1. Which of the following is *not* true of teaching for understanding?
   A. It is procedural in nature.
   B. It involves being able to repeat declarative information.
   C. It encourages higher-level thinking.
   D. It requires demonstration of understanding.

2. Which of the following is *not* a declarative objective?
   A. Students will learn vocabulary words.
   B. Students will understand the meaning of semantic memory.
   C. Students will develop a model for understanding semantic memory.
   D. Students will understand the importance of semantic memory.

3. Which of the following is an example of chunking?
   A. Read pages 17–22 in the text.
   B. Answer Questions 4–20 on the worksheet.
   C. Place your ideas for why we have world hunger in the categories provided.
   D. Choose the topic you would like to use for your project.

4. Which of the following is true of semantic memory?
   A. It is brain-compatible.
   B. It requires a great deal of intrinsic motivation.
   C. Its capacity is limitless.
   D. It is contextual in nature.

5. What is an example of procedural memory?
   A. Memorizing vocabulary
   B. Listening to lecture
   C. Watching television
   D. Driving a car

6. Which of the following is an example of episodic memory?
   A. Listening to lecture
   B. Going on a field trip
   C. Driving a car
   D. Memorizing vocabulary

7. Which of the following is an example of indirect instruction?
   A. The teacher takes the students to the library so they can do research on a given topic.
   B. The teacher introduces and explains the vocabulary words.
   C. The teacher reads a story to the children, stopping to ask questions.
   D. The teacher provides an outline on the board of the skeletal system.

8. A teacher usually uses scaffolding . . .
   A. At the conclusion of a unit.
   B. At the beginning point in learning a process.
   C. With gifted students.
   D. With visual learners.

9. Which of the following is an example of scaffolding?
   A. Students look up the definitions to their vocabulary words.
   B. Students work in small groups to define their vocabulary words.

    C. The teacher leads students in a discussion of the vocabulary words, then asks them to provide their own definitions for the words.

    D. The teacher places students in small groups and asks them to brainstorm uses of their vocabulary words.

10. When would coaching most likely *not* be used?
    A. When students are working in cooperative learning groups.
    B. When students are doing seatwork.
    C. When the teacher is lecturing.
    D. When the teacher is using a questioning technique.

11. Which of the following is an example of a declarative objective?
    A. Students will provide examples of nonlinguistic organizers.
    B. Students will develop sentences using the vocabulary provided.
    C. Students will compare and contrast parts of speech.
    D. Students will know the steps used in writing a paper.

12. Metacognition (which is **not** true) . . .
    A. Helps the brain remember the learning.
    B. Should be a part of every lesson.
    C. Can be processed through a PMI.
    D. Is a step in mastery learning.

13. Declarative objectives . . .
    A. Require the development of a model.
    B. Require knowledge and comprehension.
    C. Require movement.
    D. Require chunking.

14. Authentic learning . . .
    A. Requires rote rehearsal.
    B. Requires extrinsic rewards.

    C. Requires memorization.
    D. Requires active brain processing.

15. Which is *not* an example of explicit instruction?
    A. Cooperative learning
    B. Questioning
    C. Lecture
    D. Demonstrations

16. Procedural objectives . . .
    A. Tell the "what" of the learning.
    B. Use primarily the semantic memory system.
    C. Involve facts and vocabulary to memorize.
    D. Involve action on the part of the learner.

17. Teaching for understanding . . .
    A. Usually involves simple recall.
    B. Usually involves higher-level thinking.
    C. Usually involves only declarative objectives.
    D. Usually involves primarily at-risk students.

18. Organizers . . .
    A. Are all nonlinguistic.
    B. Are a tool for auditory learners.
    C. Are a part of meaning making.
    D. Are sequential.

19. Which is *not* an example of pedagogy?
    A. Teaching a lesson
    B. Planning a lesson
    C. Applying for a teaching job
    D. Assessing students

20. Which of the following is **not** true of metacognition?
    A. Metacognition is an activity designed to be used throughout a lesson.
    B. Metacognition can be teacher directed.
    C. Metacognition should be a part of all lessons.
    D. Metacognition has a low impact on student success.

1

Learning With Mind, Heart, and Body

While the old academic model addressed primarily the intellectual aspects of learning, the prevailing model suggests that we learn with our mind, heart and body. This more holistic view underscores the importance of considering all of the learner's issues.

—Eric Jensen, *Completing the Puzzle*

It has been said that smart people are those who can store information quickly and can retrieve it from storage quickly (Sprenger, 2002). Underachievers are those who process information quickly and retrieve it from storage slowly; overachievers are those who process information slowly but retrieve it from storage quickly. How, then, can we help students to process information in a faster and more efficient way so that on the days when they need to use the information, they can retrieve it quickly? In this chapter and the chapters to follow, we will look at ways to help students be more successful by using these activation and retrieval systems.

INCOMING INFORMATION

While most of this book deals with the cognitive system of the brain, learning does not begin there. All learning seems to begin in the self-system of the brain. This is the system that decides whether or not to engage in the learning. "If the task is judged important, if the probability of success is high, and a positive affect is generated or associated with the task, the individual will be motivated to engage in the new task" (Marzano, Pickering, & Pollock, 2001). In order to make this decision, the brain examines the incoming information in regard to the following questions:

Is the incoming information important? It is necessary to note here that information can be important to the teacher and to the students, but unless the individual student believes the information is important, this system will not view it as important. As teachers, we must not only let our students know the importance of the learning, but how it will be important to them personally. Marzano et al. (2001) explain it this way:

> What an individual considers to be important is probably a function of the extent to which it meets one of two conditions: it is perceived as instrumental in satisfying a basic need, or it is perceived as instrumental in the attainment of a personal goal.

In working with students from poverty or from the inner city, this is an especially important aspect of the learning. Merely telling these students that the learning is important because they will need it for college is probably not going to provide motivation to learn. These students tend to live in the here and now, since that is all they have. How will the information help them to survive, to keep from being cheated, or to be elevated in stature in front of their friends? In the PBS series *Good Morning, Miss Toliver*, this aspect of the self-system is handled very well. For example, when the teacher of these inner-city middle school students, Kay Toliver, is teaching fractions, she uses the example of pizza slices. Knowing fractional parts will help her students to judge which pizza slice is the best buy.

Have I had success in the past with this type of learning? One of the most important aspects of the self-system is self-efficacy. Self-efficacy is the belief that one can do something because of past success. This is somewhat different from self-esteem, which is the belief in oneself. Self-efficacy is based on concrete proof, not just "I think" and "I feel." For this reason it is important that we provide opportunities for students to experience success—even in incremental steps. The old adage "Success breeds success," is absolutely true. Marzano (2001) expands self-efficacy to say that it includes not only ability but also power and the necessary resources to be successful. Consistency in providing the necessary prerequisite skills and the necessary resources for success prior to an assignment helps to build self-efficacy in our students. How can we do this? Never give an assignment in which you will take a grade without providing the following:

- A matrix or rubric or other written form that tells students exactly what they must do to be successful. When we do this, there are no "gotchas" in the learning. Students don't need to guess our expectations, and they are more assured that there will be consistency in grading. In my book *What Every Teacher Should Know About Student Assessment*, I talk about how to build a matrix and a rubric. Form 1.1 is an example of a matrix for math homework. The information on the left-hand side contains the categories involved in the assignment. The checklist on the right contains the attributes that make the assignment a quality product.

Form 1.1   Homework Matrix

Components of the Assignment	Point Value	Characteristics of Quality
Problem solving		❑ Problem written correctly ❑ All work shown ❑ Work is neat and easy to read
Answers to problems		❑ Correctly answered ❑ Work has been checked for accuracy
Overall quality of work		❑ Work is handed in on time ❑ Work is legible ❑ Work shows evidence of thought

- Adequate time to practice the learning. Jensen (1997) says it is important for the brain to know that it knows the learning. We help the brain to know by providing information in various modalities (auditory, visual, and kinesthetic) and by practicing the learning sufficiently in terms of number of times practiced and time provided for the practice.

- Specific feedback. By specific feedback I mean feedback that not only tells students the strengths of their work but the weaknesses as well. Specific feedback provides dialogue on how the student is doing in regard to learner goals and classroom goals. Specific feedback offers suggestions and leads students to problem solve when things are not going well or when they reach an impasse in the learning. Avoid blanket statements like "Good job" because these statements do little to improve learning.

- How do I feel about the learning (classroom, teacher, other students, and subject matter)? If you have ever been in a classroom in which the emotional climate was one of tension or fear, you already know why this aspect of learning is so important. Our species has survived because our brain attends to information by priority. If we are under threat, whether physical, emotional, or otherwise, our brain pays attention to the threat over all other incoming stimuli. As Jensen (1997) says,

The brain stem is the part of the brain that directs your behavior under negative stress; and is the most responsive to any threat. When threat is perceived, excessive cortisol is released into the body causing higher-order thinking to take a backseat to automatic functions that may help you survive.

Jensen (1997) places threats into categories that assist in our understanding of how threat affects the classroom (our brain likes information in categories or other patterns). The following categories are presented with an analysis (by me) of how they might affect our classrooms.

Potential Physical Harm. We cannot control most of the physical threats our students may receive outside the classroom, but we certainly have control over the seven to eight hours that they are within our classrooms. Set class norms and include in your classroom specific instruction on working with others. Insist that students are respectful of others and never tolerate put-downs or remarks that could be deemed as racial, sexual, or hurtful in nature.

Intellectual Threats. These threats occur when students' ideas are laughed at or put down. They also occur when students do not know the answer or give an incorrect answer. While it is impossible to prevent incorrect answers, you can create a climate in your classroom that says it is OK if you don't know the answer. What is not OK is not to try. When you ask questions, be sure that you provide adequate wait time and that the wait time is consistent. For example, it is easy to cut short the wait time for a reluctant learner and to provide more wait time for a student who usually knows the answer. Try counting to yourself to be sure that you give the same amount of time to all students. Also, accept and compliment partial answers or the part of the answer that was correct. Remember the information provided earlier on self-efficacy? If you are having trouble with student motivation, self-efficacy is probably at the heart of the problem.

Emotional Threats. One of the greatest fears of adolescents is the fear of being embarrassed in front of peers. In the past, due to behavioral psychology that used a system of rewards and punishments, teachers often used this type of threat to control students. We now know that the downside is not worth any of the positives from this philosophy. Once you embarrass an adolescent, you will create an enemy in the classroom and someone who will not learn to potential.

Cultural-Social Threats. Don't allow or participate in disrespect for any one group in the classroom. Isolating students or putting students in groups according to ethnicity is another way that we show bias in the classroom. Teachers often show cultural bias by including only materials and information that show one race or that show only males or females in specific roles.

Resource Restriction. This type of threat occurs when we do not provide adequate tools, time, or resources to carry out assignments. State and national testing has lead to a nation that is trying to "cover the material for the test" instead of making sure that students understand before moving on.

While we want students to experience some stress in the classroom (e.g., from work that is challenging), we do not want them to experience negative stress or stress over time. Gazzaniga (1992) says, "It's not stress that's bad, it's uncontrollable stress that's bad."

PROCESSING INFORMATION

Once the brain has decided to pay attention to the incoming information, the metacognitive system takes over. This is the system that sets goals for the learning and that monitors the progress of the learning. This system is important if the student is to complete a task or engage in the learning over time. If a student has difficulty understanding or completing a task, it is this system that decides whether to problem solve or simply acquiesce. As teachers, we can assist this system of the brain by:

1. Setting goals for the learning (based on state and national goals) and providing those goals in a format so that our students know the expectation. I like to post the goals in the room so that my students can see them. College students get a copy of the goals for each lesson. For young students, I recommend that the goals be sent home to parents in an informative letter. By doing this, I am modeling the process and I am making my students aware that they are working toward goals that are deemed important.

2. Next, ask students to set personal goals. Remember that the learning has to have personal meaning to the learners. From time to time ask students to review their personal goals to help them examine their own progress. You might use a notebook for setting goals or a simple model like the one in Form 1.2.

3. Provide specific and consistent feedback to students to help them identify where they are in terms of goals.

4. Directly teach students how to problem solve, so that when they are not meeting their learning goals they can change direction or determine changes that need to be made in order to be specific. Payne (2001) says that an effective way to deal with students from poverty is to get them to write down what they did, what went wrong, and what they will do differently next time. While Payne was talking specifically about dealing with behavior problems, this same technique can help students learn to monitor and adjust their work. Model for your students how you use positive self-talk to help when they are having difficulty with learning. For example, a math teacher might show students how to work a math problem by using a step-by-step process and then what to do when a mistake is made, using self-talk to work through the process. Students tend to know a great deal about negative self-talk but may not have been exposed to this powerful tool when it is put in a positive context.

THE COGNITIVE SYSTEM

Most of what we do in the classroom revolves around the cognitive system of the brain. According to Marzano (1998), the cognitive system is organized into four categories:

1. Storage and retrieval: "The storage and retrieval processes provide an individual with access to the knowledge that has been stored in permanent memory

Form 1.2   Sample Model for Setting Goals

Unit Eight: The Boston Tea Party

State Goals: Students will understand events in history in the context of the times

Students will connect events in history with human behavior

As we look at this important event in history and its significance to the Revolutionary War, what are your personal goals for the unit? To write your goals, think about what you already know about the Boston Tea Party and the Revolutionary War. What would you like to know about this event? What do you need to know about this event?

My personal goals are:

and a way of storing new knowledge so that it might be issued at a later date" (Marzano, 1998).

2. Information processing: "The information processing functions manipulate knowledge that has been stored so that it might be utilized for specific tasks" (Marzano, 1998).

3. Input/output: These functions use knowledge to understand communication through hearing, writing, reading, and so on, with the outside world.

4. Knowledge use: This part of the cognitive system uses knowledge to carry out specific tasks. Procedural goals are carried out through this part of the cognitive system.

These categories within the cognitive system will be discussed as we look at how the brain takes in information, processes it, sends it to long-term storage, and then retrieves it when needed.

2

How Do We Acquire and Process Information?

Our rate of learning is the amount of time it takes to acquire information. It is rate of learning that seems to distinguish slow learners from the typical learner. Slow learners seem to have difficulty taking in information for processing. These students often need re-teaching and frequent reinforcement in order to process and store the learning. In this chapter, we will examine ways to help all students take in information more efficiently and ways the classroom teacher can assist students as they make decisions about what information to store and what to delete from the brain's processing systems. While most of this process is automatic, there are certain tactics that we can use to ensure students are more likely to retain the learning.

Information comes to us through the senses and then goes to the thalamus for sorting. Visual information is sorted and sent to the visual part of the cortex, auditory information is

Figure 2.1

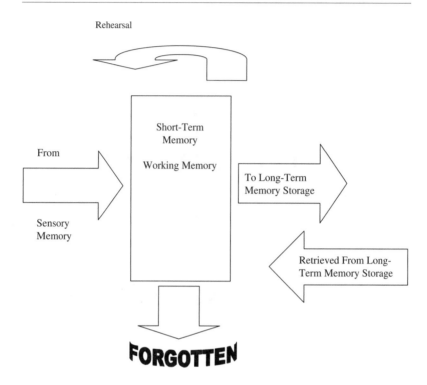

sent to the auditory cortex, and so it goes. In the cerebral cortex, important decisions are made about whether to act on the information, send it to long-term memory, or just delete it. The graphic in Figure 2.1 shows how we acquire most (about 99%) of our information and the processes that new information goes through before being stored.

Most brain researchers say that 99% of what we learn comes to us through our senses; that is, through vision, hearing, smelling, tasting, and touching. Sousa (1995) says our brains take in about 40,000 bits per second through the senses. Wow! That means that the classroom environment is important and that the way teachers teach students is important in helping students acquire and use information. Step back in your mind and visualize your classroom as if you were standing at the door looking in. What do you see? Smell? Hear? So often in the classroom we rely on the auditory and ignore most of the rest of the senses. An enriched classroom takes into account all of the senses in learning. Jensen (1997) says that at least 87% of the learners in the classroom do not learn just by hearing. They must see the learning in a visual format and/or experience the learning kinesthetically. I have been convinced for some time that we could raise the mathematics scores of students all over this country today if we could find more ways to show students how math works. Jensen's research shows that for 87% of the students, just memorizing the formulas is not enough. Most of the teaching in the classroom is done through one or more of three modalities that use the senses: visual, auditory, and kinesthetic. For slow learners, it is critical that the learning is in a modality that is comfortable for them. In other words, if you have been teaching your class auditorily, without visuals or kinesthetic opportunities, and you have a group of students who do not understand, you must re-teach them in a different modality.

Jensen and others have identified three learning modalities found in all of us. Most of us prefer one of these modalities to the others and are able to take in information faster and more efficiently if we are taught in our preferred modality. As a matter of fact, it is believed that students who have difficulty with the learning and must be re-taught will not be successful unless they are re-taught in the modality in which they learn best. Here are the three modalities and a brief explanation of each.

Visual Learners

The visual learners make up the largest group in the classroom. These learners need to "see" the learning before it will make sense to them. It is important to have visuals for these learners so they can see the information. They need pictures, graphic organizers, information posted in the room, and opportunities to reflect through visualization. I had an interesting experience with a first grader who was very visual and was not being taught in his preferred modality. I had volunteered to teach two first grade classes for about 45 minutes while the two teachers collaborated on a project. Both classes were brought to the library where I was to read them a wonderful book, *Dinorella*. When the teachers brought the students in, one of the teachers whispered to me that one little boy (who was sitting off by himself) would probably be a discipline problem. She explained that he could not sit still for a story and might have to be taken out of the room. Instead of just reading the story, I had made pictures of some of the pages and put them on PowerPoint so that the children could all see the pictures as I read. Not only was the boy in question sitting on the edge of his chair throughout the story, but when I finished he slapped his knee and said, "Do it again." This is an example of a visual learner who can become a discipline problem if he cannot see the learning. At the secondary level, how many students drop out mentally when they are not being taught in the modality most comfortable to their brains? The less students are able to control their actions, the more likely this will happen.

Tileston (2000) provides these characteristics of visual learners. Visual learners

- Have difficulty remembering names but may remember details about the person.
- Learn best when there are visual tools to help explain the learning.
- Would rather read a story themselves than have someone read it to them.
- Organize thoughts by writing them down.
- Have difficulty remembering directions that are told to them.
- Often give away their emotions through their facial expressions.
- Like puzzles and other visual tools.

Figure 2.2

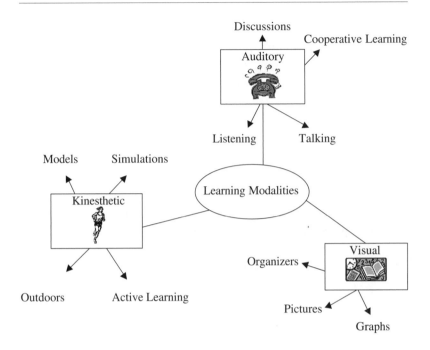

By adding visual stimulus to the classroom, we provide opportunities for these learners to be more successful. Remember that for these learners it is important to see the learning. One idea for the classroom follows:

Teach students to use nonlinguistic organizers. Non-linguistic organizers are visual maps that use few words but include symbols, colors, and designs to help students organize the information. Figure 2.2 is an example of a visual organizer that can be used for different purposes in the learning. This mind map is an example of a visual tool that is a powerful way to help students not only see the learning, but put it into an organized format for the brain. Figure 2.2 is a mind map of the three learning modalities that we are discussing. See if this visual tool helps you to understand the modalities better. If so, you may be a visual learner.

Auditory Learners

Auditory learners make up the smallest number in the classroom. Perhaps it is our multimedia world that has diminished the number of students who prefer to learn by sitting and listening. For these students, hearing the information either through lecture, discussion, or media is important to the brain, but they must also be given opportunities to talk. Sprenger (2002) says, "When these students read text, and sometimes they don't, you will often see them moving their lips or mumbling. In fact, these learners have a tendency to talk to themselves." She goes on to explain that auditory information is sometimes stored in sequence and must be retrieved in sequence for these students. Sprenger uses the example of learning the alphabet by memorizing the alphabet song. Now, we all know the alphabet, but what if someone asks you to quickly tell him or her the letter that comes after *h?* Do you need to go through the alphabet song to get to the *h* before you can answer? Sprenger says, "Auditory learners encounter that problem on a test when the questions are not in the same order in which the material was presented." Since learning in the past was primarily by auditory methods, teachers who rely almost completely on auditory teaching will probably have difficulty with students from other modalities, especially kinesthetic learners.

Tileston (2000) provides this description of auditory learners. Auditory learners:

- Remember names better than faces
- Fidget in the classroom when made to sit for long periods of time
- Forget what is read unless it is discussed
- Respond to physical encouragement such as a pat on the back
- Would rather be in a group discussion about a topic than read about it
- Are cognizant of the temperature and comfort level of the room, and are affected by those characteristics

- Are easily distracted by sounds
- Are good storytellers
- Prefer to give oral reports rather than written work

KINESTHETIC LEARNERS

Sprenger (2002) says, "Every lesson should contain movement. Take that movement and repeat it often enough and it becomes a permanent memory. Along with that movement, the learning associated with it becomes permanent." As a matter of fact, teachers who rely heavily on lecture for teaching will probably have a great deal of difficulty with kinesthetic learners. These learners need to move, and they need models of the learning that they can hold and touch. According to Jensen (1997), sitting for long stretches of time in a structured environment may be brain-unfriendly. The brain seems to be designed to be able to pay attention for short stretches of time but not for long periods. "The reticular formation near the top of the brain stem and base of the limbic system is the part of our brain that integrates incoming sensory information. Using peptide receptors, it regulates our general level of attention." This is a good thing, because if we paid attention to all incoming stimulus, we would be in overload. Jensen (1997) goes on to say,

> Although the brain is very good at immediate change and contrasts, it is poor at discerning slow trends. Thus the design seems to be for the short-term. This provides us with a biological explanation of why expecting extended classroom attention is problematic and even inappropriate.

These students need to have hands-on activities, and they need to practice the learning in order for it to make sense to them. They may even say, "Don't give me a lot of directions, just give me the work and let me do it."

I sometimes volunteer to teach in various classrooms. One day when I was scheduled to teach in a high school class about the brain and modalities, several other teachers asked if they could bring their classes in as well. We wound up with about 75 students in a large classroom. Students were sitting everywhere, including at my feet. At the conclusion of the class, a student walked up to me and asked if I knew who he was. I said that I did. He has been in commercials and on magazine covers. He said that what I did not know about him was that he was diagnosed with attention-deficit/hyperactive disorder. He went on to tell me that he had to be medicated in order to be able to sit quietly in school and take notes. He said that if only teachers would teach to all modalities, including kinesthetic, maybe he would not have to be medicated so much. While I do believe that ADHD is a very real and frustrating phenomenon, I strongly agree that if we would add more movement to the classroom, we might not have so many of these students struggling.

Tileston (2000) offers this description of kinesthetic learners. Kinesthetic learners:

- Remember best what was done rather than what was seen or heard
- When faced with a problem, will often choose the solution that involves the most activity
- Would rather participate in almost anything than just watch
- Like simulations, drama, and outdoor activity
- Like models and will often build models for independent projects
- Give away their emotions through their body language

The key is to provide a variety of teaching techniques that take into account that students need to hear, to see, and to move. Teach modalities to your students so that they know their strengths and weaknesses. Provide ideas to help them control impulsivity and lack of motivation by recognizing when the learning is not in their modality. Also, provide a variety of tools for students to use to help them make the learning meaningful. For example, directly teach your students how to use nonlinguistic and linguistic organizers to help them organize the learning.

THE PERCEPTUAL REGISTER

It is the perceptual register or reticular activation system (RAS) that helps the brain deal with all of the incoming data. This powerful system monitors incoming information and quickly decides whether it is worthy of our attention. Without this filtering system, you could not sit outside and read—you would be so bombarded by birds chirping, bees buzzing by, animal noises, the wind blowing your hair, and more, that you could not read. Because you do have this system working for you, these sensory stimuli are blocked out so that you can attend to what is important to you at the time. According to Anderson (1995),

> If the information in sensory memory is not encoded in the brief time before it decays, it is lost. What subjects encode depends on what they are paying attention to. The environment typically offers much more information at one time than we can attend to and encode. Therefore, much of what enters our sensory system results in no permanent record.

The brain discards about 98% of all incoming messages. On the upside, that is a good thing because if we remembered everything that came into our brain, we would all be on sensory overload and couldn't focus. The downside is that sometimes we discard information that we need to remember. This explains, in part, why students cannot remember all that information we give to them. It was never stored in long-term memory.

SHORT-TERM MEMORY

On test day, students will often come into the classroom and say, "Hurry, hurry and give me the test before I forget the information." Those students do not know the material, they are merely saying it over and over (about every 15 seconds) so that they can hold it in short-term memory long enough to write it on the test. Ask them the same question next week, and they will not remember the information. This is much like going to the telephone directory to look up a number we need to call. We say the number over and over to keep it in short-term memory long enough to complete the call. Once the call has been placed, short-term memory deletes it because it is not perceived as important. Short-term memory, then, is another filter through which the stimuli must pass on the way to long-term memory. Up to this point, the processes of the brain have been filtering unconsciously. As information enters the working memory, conscious processing begins.

WORKING MEMORY

Once information enters the working memory, we have about 15 seconds while the brain decides to process the information or to discard it—about 98% of the information is discarded at this point. How, then, do we ever get information into long-term memory? The key to getting information into long-term memory is rehearsal. As long as working memory is "doing something" with the learning, it can hold it there indefinitely. Rehearsal refers to what we do with the information once it has been introduced into working memory through the senses or retrieved from long-term storage. Rehearsal performs two functions; it maintains information in working memory, and it is the mechanism by which we transfer information to long-term memory. Both the amount of time devoted to the rehearsal and the type of rehearsal are important. Rehearsal may be rote or elaborate.

1. Rote rehearsal refers to the deliberate, continuous repetition of material in the same form in which it entered short-term memory. Rote rehearsal is used when the learner needs to remember and store information exactly as it is entered into working memory. Examples include math facts, spelling, and state capitals.

2. Elaborative rehearsal involves elaborating on or integrating information, giving it some kind of sense or meaning. In elaborative rehearsal the learner does something with the information. Elaborative rehearsal is used when it is not necessary to store information exactly as learned, but when it is more important to associate the new learnings with prior learnings to detect relationships. Examples include problem solving, vocabulary in context, and reading comprehension.

INFORMATION PROCESSING

The information processing function of the cognitive structure of the brain acts on the data in working memory. This process takes place regardless of whether stimuli are coming in from the outside world or whether data are being retrieved from long-term memory. Marzano (1998) provides six basic information-processing functions that may take place at this time. We will examine them one at a time.

Matching. The brain may look at the information to identify similarities and differences between it and information stored in long-term memory. Simply put, the brain may ask, "What do I already know or what have I already experienced that will help me attach the new learning?" In their studies of the meta-analysis of instructional practices, McREL and Marzano (1998) found that the teaching practice of associating the new learning with something the students already know or have experienced will make a significant difference in the learning. Asking students to find similarities or differences between two or more subjects can raise the understanding at this point by 40 percentile points. In other words, a student working at the 50th percentile who effectively identifies similarities and differences as a part of the learning process can move to the 90th percentile at this point. For example, if you are teaching a unit on amphibians and reptiles, you might use Form 2.1 to help your students identify how the two are alike (in terms of

Form 2.1   Similarities/Differences

Directions: For the graphic model below, write the characteristics of reptiles and amphibians that are alike. On the left-hand side write in the characteristics of amphibians that are different from those of reptiles. On the right-hand side, write the characteristics of reptiles that are different from amphibians. For example, both amphibians and reptiles are hatched from eggs, but amphibians change as they mature. Reptiles remain the same as they mature.

Amphibians	Common Characteristics	Reptiles
Change as they mature		Stay the same as they mature
	Hatched from eggs	
	Cold blooded	

attributes) and how they are different. According to research, this one tool can help raise your students understanding by as much as 40 percentile points (Marzano, 1998).

Idea Representation. According to Marzano "Idea representation is the process of translating the data in working memory into a form suitable for storage in permanent memory." We do not store information in exactly the same way that it came into the system but rather in the way that we interpret the data. This explains, in part, why students may learn information incorrectly. The data were taken in through the senses (usually by reading or hearing) and processed in working memory according to the learner's interpretation. Data may be represented by the learner as linguistic, nonlinguistic, or affective at this time. Two learners will not necessarily interpret the data in the same way. We can help our students to process information correctly by using both linguistic and nonlinguistic organizers in the classroom. A linguistic organizer would include such tools as a learning log, a graph or model of the learning, or any structure that helps students organize the information using words. A nonlinguistic organizer is a visual model that uses a minimum of words but relies on symbols, colors, and the like, such as might be used on a mind map. The meta-analysis study from McREL (see Marzano, 1998) on effective teaching practices shows that when teachers use graphic representations, such as a mind map at this stage in the learning, a student working at the 50th percentile range can be moved to the 89th percentile. When we consider that the 50th percentile is not a mastery level in any state and that the 89th percentile is above the mastery level, this has great significance in terms of student performance.

Information Screening. This function of working memory looks at the data to see if they are reasonable. If they are not deemed reasonable, the individual will not accept the data. Not only must the data make sense, they must make sense to learners in regard to what they already know or have experienced. If the information is thought to be unreasonable, there is a strong chance that it may be deleted at this point. The implication is that we must help our students to see the reasonableness of the learning so that it is not screened out of working memory.

Information Generalization. This function looks for general rules that can be applied to the information as compared to general rules already stored in long-term memory. For example, a student working a new math problem will look for general rules that apply to working the new problem based on general rules that have been used in the past. If the rule is new or if the rule negates a rule in long-term memory, it may be necessary to monitor and change the rule in long-term memory during this function.

Information Specification. During this process, deductions are formed based on the new learning and past experiences or learning. For example, "If an object is a large slender dog with very long white and gold hair, then it is a collie" (Marzano, 1998). The effect of information specification and information generalization on student achievement is relatively low, which indicates that teachers might use their time more wisely in idea representation during processing rather than asking students to infer generalizations from specific observations or pieces of information (information generalization), or make predictions based on known pieces of information, as in information specification. At last, we truly can work smarter, not harder.

Idea Production. This function creates new ideas using information from long-term memory. For example, while sitting on the porch reading a book, the learner might create ideas from the reading and information in long-term storage that are new to the learner. The ideas might be communicated to others or they might be kept to oneself. In the writing process, this area is activated when students gather their ideas or thoughts to put into words on paper.

In summary: Each brain is unique, and yet there are some activities that are common to all of us. We take in 99% of our information through the senses. Our brain decides very quickly whether the information is worthy of rehearsal and thus long-term memory, or if it should be discarded. Most information coming in through the senses is discarded. The upside of that is that if the brain stored every piece of incoming information, we would all be on information overload. The downside is that our students often toss out some of the information that we had hoped they would remember.

We take in information primarily in three ways (visual, auditory, kinesthetic) and we have preferences for how we take in the new learning. Slow learners must be re-taught in their preferred modality for the learning to make sense to them.

We use rehearsal to store information in long-term memory. There are two types of rehearsal:

1. Rote rehearsal works well for the psychomotor domain/ procedural pathway learning, but not for the semantic pathway, declarative knowledge.

2. Elaborate rehearsal works for declarative knowledge by giving it some kind of meaning. The brain constructs meaning through relevance, emotion, and the use of patterns or connections.

Think about your classroom. What do you have students *do* with new information?

3

Working Memory

In Chapters 1 and 2, we explored how the brain takes in information and the processes involved before the information is sent to long-term memory storage. In this chapter, we will look at what happens in working memory and the factors that contribute to the brain's decision to move information into long-term storage.

As I discussed in Chapter 1, most learning enters the brain through the senses. There are three modalities primarily involved in the process: auditory, which is processed and stored in the temporal lobes on the sides of the brain near the ears; visual, which is stored in the occipital lobe at the back of the brain; and kinesthetic, which is stored at the top of the brain in the motor cortex and later in the cerebellum. Once the information enters the brain through the various modalities, it is held in the association cortex until it is either tossed out, sent to working memory, or sent to long-term memory (Sprenger, 1999). Once new learning has been registered through the perceptual or sensory register in the brain stem, it moves to temporary memory, which is made up of short-term memory (an extension of the perceptual register) and working memory, where processing occurs (Sousa, 2001). Working

Figure 3.1

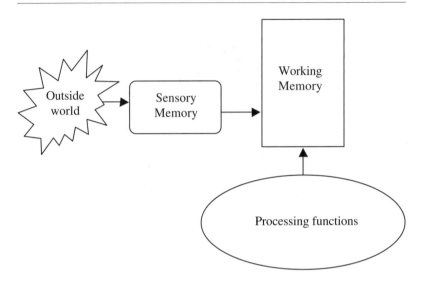

memory holds information for about 15 seconds while it decides whether to toss it or move it along. Figure 3.1 graphically shows the path taken thus far by the incoming information.

At this point in the process, the brain is making an important decision—whether to move the information into long-term storage or to toss it out as unimportant. As teachers, we hope that our students will send the information into long-term storage because we know that we cannot recall what we do not have in storage. At this point the brain asks, "Does the information make sense? And does it have meaning for me?" Let's look at these two crucial factors and how the classroom teacher can facilitate a positive answer for both questions.

MEANING

Of the two questions, Sousa (2001) says, "Does the information have meaning?" has the most impact on whether the information will be moved to long-term storage. He uses the example of television shows that we watch for pleasure.

The program may make sense, but it usually does not have personal meaning for us so we do not remember the details. On the other hand, if we watch a television show that reminds us of a personal experience or one from which we gain insight into solving a personal problem, we will more likely put it into long-term storage.

We cannot create meaning for our students; each one of us must create our own meaning. A good teacher, however, knows how to create the environment that facilitates meaning. According to Jensen (1997) and others, there are three ways that the brain constructs meaning.

1. Through relevance. Jensen says, "In order for learning to be considered relevant, it must relate to something the learner already knows. It must activate a learner's existing neural networks. The more relevance, the greater the meaning." For example, a teacher introducing the book *Snowed In at Pokeweed Public School* by Bianchi might begin by asking students what they would do if they had to spend the night at school. The teacher might give them some choices such as: play games, sing, do art activities, cry for their parents, and so on. These are the same choices the students at Pokeweed face when they are snowed in overnight. By making the learning relevant to the students first, the teacher has opened the way to better understanding by the students. To begin a unit on estimation, a teacher might bring to class a jar of marbles as part of a contest to guess the number of marbles in the jar for a prize. Begin by asking the students for ideas about how to estimate how many marbles are in the jar. Most students love games and are more likely to participate in the lesson if they see how estimation is used from the beginning.

2. Through emotion. Emotion is the strongest force for embedding into long-term memory in the brain; it has the power to shut down our thinking or to strengthen an experience so that we remember it for life. We add

emotion to the learning through music (try adding sounds of the times to lessons), celebrations of the learning, and by adding visuals, simulations, and real-world applications. My brother, who majored in pharmacy and works for a major drug company, told me recently that everything he ever needed to know to be successful he learned in second grade. His second grade teacher, Mrs. Eggars, understood how to use emotion in the classroom brilliantly. He told me that when all of the other second grade classes were studying a country like Italy, that they brought in some of the food of the country one day, showed some of the costumes another day, and so on. Not his classroom; his classroom was Italy. It looked like, smelled like, tasted like, and sounded like Italy. She even introduced them to Italian opera. According to Jensen, "When the learner's emotions are engaged, the brain codes the content by triggering the release of chemicals that single out and mark the experience as important and meaningful. Emotions activate many areas in the body and the brain, including the prefrontal cortices, amygdala, hippocampus and often the stomach."

3. Through patterns or connections. The brain is a seeker of connections; it is constantly asking, "What do I already know about this subject that can be connected to the new information?" Thus it is important that a part of rehearsal includes connections to prior learning. Whenever we throw new information to the brain, there is a moment of chaos while the brain asks, "What do I already know that applies to this?" For example, in introducing a new unit on statistics, a wise teacher will review some basic algebra facts that students will need in order to connect the new learning. What if the students do not have any prior knowledge of the subject? For example, in the book about the students at Pokeweed, it is safe to say that the students in the classroom have not ever had to stay overnight at school, so they will not know what that is like. By creating empathy

for the students by asking students to make choices about what they might do, we are developing a personal connection for them. In my book, *Ten Best Teaching Strategies*, I use the illustration of a teacher about to teach a unit on immigration. The teacher does not assume that students will know and understand why anyone would get in an inner tube and risk their lives to come to this country, so the teacher begins by saying, "What would have to happen in this country to cause you to pick up whatever you could carry in your arms and to go to a country in which you know no one?" Students will discuss for a time and then the teacher will say, "What would have to happen in this country on the religious front? On the medical front? What would have to happen economically? Politically?" By doing this, not only does the teacher build a connection up-front for the new learning but helps students to look at information from new perspectives. They are using elaborative rehearsal.

MAKING SENSE OF THE LEARNING

It is possible for information to have meaning to the brain but not make sense; it is also possible for information to make sense to the brain and not have meaning. We have said that of the two, it is more important for the information to have meaning. It is also possible for the brain to send information to long-term storage that makes sense but has no personal meaning, i.e., trivia. According to Sousa (1995), "Some neuropsychologists estimate that up to 10% of what we have in long-term storage may have been acquired in this way." That explains why some of us can pull an unfamiliar word out of long-term storage while doing crossword puzzles.

In your classroom, what are some things that you do to ensure that the new learning has meaning and that it makes sense?

4

Long-Term
Memory
Pathways

A ccording to Sousa (1995),

> Long-term memory refers to the process of storing and
> retrieving information. Long-term storage refers to where
> in the brain the memories are kept. Think of the long-term
> storage sites as a library and of long-term memory as a
> librarian who retrieves information and returns it to its
> proper storage places.

For the purposes of this chapter, we will look at the storage
system itself and at ways to retrieve information with greater
efficiency.

MEMORY PATHWAYS

Most researchers include three memory pathways through
which information is stored in long-term memory. While most

learning in the classroom is directed toward the semantic pathway, educators should strive to incorporate all three pathways to make the learning more powerful and to help students do a better job of retrieving information.

THE SEMANTIC MEMORY SYSTEM

This is the memory system most often used in education. It is the area that stores words and facts—and it is the least brain-compatible of the three memory systems. That is one of the reasons our students cannot remember the learning. When facts and words are taught in isolation, without any context or connection, they are lost unless rehearsed, reviewed, or relearned. Teaching English language learners using this memory system is unproductive since these students lack the language skills to be able to make meaning of the learning. The same is true of students from poverty. Most of their learning outside of school and prior to entering school has been contextual and has involved semantic memory in a very limited way. Jensen (1997) says,

> The exact location of the semantic memory function has not been pinpointed, though we know it operates out of the cerebral cortex. The brain is poorly designed for remembering print and text copy. Information embedded in content is usually learned, or attempted to be learned, through rote tactics and by following list-like formats. Semantic memory is the type of list-oriented, sometimes rote, memory which requires rehearsal; it is resistant to change, is isolated from context, has strict limits, lacks meaning and is linked to extrinsic motivation.

In other words, if students are to learn facts and words, they must have something with which to connect that information, otherwise it is useless to the brain and discarded. Some techniques that help students to remember facts or words include mnemonics (Please Excuse My Dear Aunt

Sally, for operations in math), rhymes (remember how you learned the alphabet with a song?), peg words or past learning with similar content (Last week we learned . . . this week we will add to that by learning . . .). As Jensen says, "This type of learning is typified by seated classroom work and homework, e.g., 'Study for Friday's test by reading chapter six.'"

The capacity of semantic memory is restricted. We have difficulty dealing with large amounts of semantic facts at one time. That may account for the reason so many of our students say, "When are we ever going to use this?" Their brains are in overload, and if they are not going to use the information, why tack it onto the frustration they are already feeling? One way that we can add more information into semantic memory is by chunking the information into some type of category system. For example, instead of giving my students a long list of why people immigrate, I give them categories of reasons such as religious reasons, political reasons, economic reasons, social reasons, and so on. By doing this, I am helping them to put the information into a format that is more brain friendly and that will allow us to cover more reasons. The average adult can handle about seven to ten chunks of new information at one time. A three-year-old child can handle about one chunk of information at a time. That is one of the reasons we give small children only one direction at a time: "Pick up your blocks." If we said, "Pick up your blocks and take them to your room. Put them in your toy box and close the lid," the chances are the child would only get through the first direction. The amount of chunks of information that we can process at one time is age dependent and is fixed. (We cannot change the number of chunks, although we can change how much we put into a chunk.) Form 4.1 is based on several pieces of research from Sousa, Jensen, and others. It shows the number of chunks of information that we can handle at a given age.

What does this mean for the learner? It means that if I give my high school students 20 unrelated items to learn, they will have difficulty with the processing because their brains are

Form 4.1   Chunking and Age

Age of the Student	Number of Chunks (approximate)
15- adult	7–10
13	6
11	5
9	4
7	3
5	2
3	1

wired to process 7 to 10 chunks of information at one time. Let's say that for the unit on immigration, I give my students 20 unrelated reasons why people immigrate. This is much more difficult to learn than if I give them seven categories of reasons why people immigrate, such as religion, economics, social, medical, education, political, and climate.

Now, all 20 of my reasons can be incorporated into the categories—I have just made the learning easier to process by putting it into categories or chunks. I can't change the number of items that the brain can process at once, but I can change the amount of information that it can process by chunking related items. Remember that the brain likes patterns, so anything that I can do to help my students chunk or place information into patterns helps them to remember semantic information. Mind maps are another example of a powerful way to help students process factual information.

RETRIEVING FROM SEMANTIC MEMORY

I have already said that semantic memory needs a connector. Our brain is not built to store meaningless information or long strings of data without something to connect it to. So many times my students will say, "I know I know that, I just can't remember." The information may, in fact, be in storage, but the student may not be able to retrieve it. We can help our students by providing some type of connection for the facts, information, dates, places, people, and more, that we want them to remember. Here are some suggestions to get you started:

- Use nonlinguistic organizers such as the mind map to help students organize and remember the learning.
- Use peer teaching in which students are paired with another student to review information. One of the ways I do this is to stop at intervals and ask my students to tell each other what they remember from the information they have just been given. If you like to teach using lecture, this is a good way to break up the lecture and to help students "chunk" the information.
- Put the information into manageable chunks by classifying or categorizing long lists.
- Use questioning strategies like Socratic Questioning to help students process the information.
- Make your room reflect the unit you are studying. Elementary teachers do a good job of this, but somewhere between middle school and high school this technique becomes lost. Just changing the room to visually reflect each unit helps the brain sort the information.
- Wear hats or use symbols with the learning to help students remember. For example, I use picture frames when we are talking about frames of reference. Sometimes when my students cannot remember, just saying, "Remember, it was on the blue picture frame" will help to trigger this memory system.
- Use mnemonics or stories to weave the information into. On a recent new show, students participating in the national memory contest were asked how they remember all of the trivia and data they are given to memorize. One student said, "We weave a story around it to help us remember."
- Use music. Music leaves such a strong emotional impression on each of us. Bring in music to introduce and reinforce learning in the classroom.

Form 4.2   Organizer for Math Class

Math Unit	Formulas	Explanation	Example of Use

- Use linguistic organizers to help your students with the learning. For example, to help students remember the various math concepts that you will study, you might provide an organizer such as the one in Form 4.2.

THE EPISODIC MEMORY SYSTEM

The episodic memory system is based on context and location (where were you when you learned the material or in what context did you learn the information?). While this memory system is used in the early elementary years, its use diminishes each year as the student moves through the education system until it is rarely used in secondary school except in the arts or vocational classes. This memory system, located in the hippocampus, is highly brain-compatible, and information can be remembered for years (although details may become distorted unless they are reviewed from time to time). It is this memory system that allows us to remember events in history many years after they occur. For example, many people can tell you where they were when they heard that President Kennedy had been shot or when Dr. King was shot. Some can tell you who else was present and may even know what they were wearing at the time. The details get distorted over time, but the main facts remain intact. The information is remembered because it is remembered in context, and it has a strong emotional tie. The two are powerful. We can tap into this system by teaching students information in context and by adding emotions to the learning. Simulations, drama, debates, and discussions are ways to activate this system. Add emotion through music, movement, smells, visuals, and stories. Use visuals often with the learning. Remember that at least 87% of learners need visuals. Contextual learning is essential when we work with students from poverty. These students often lack the vocabulary skills to learn through the semantic system, but they have experience in learning through story-telling (which is a part of the episodic memory system). Teachers who work with students from poverty will do well to explore this memory system and how to incorporate it into the classroom. Because students today are often not motivated intrinsically, this is a good memory system because it requires little intrinsic motivation to be activated. By combining this memory system with the words and facts needed by the semantic memory system, teachers can help students not only to review information, but also to remember it.

Add to that the fact that the episodic memory system is unlimited in storage capacity. Where the semantic memory system is limited by chunks (7–10 for an adult), the episodic memory system requires little intrinsic motivation to store information and can remember large amounts of information for years—forever, if it is rehearsed periodically.

RETRIEVING FROM EPISODIC MEMORY

The episodic memory system is more easily activated than the semantic memory system. However, you can help students activate semantic information by combining it with episodic strategies. Here are some ways to help students activate the episodic memory system.

1. Put information up so that it is visually accessible to the learners who need visuals to learn well. Visuals are critical for ELL (English language learner) students' learning because they have limited semantic (language) acquisition strategies.

2. Color-code units or use symbols, especially if there is a great deal of vocabulary involved.

3. Use graphic (nonlinguistic) organizers to help students "see" the learning, and teach students to develop graphic organizers of their own for learning.

4. Change the room arrangement prior to a new unit. (This technique affects context—"Remember we talked about that information when you were all seated facing the windows.")

5. Use symbols and/or costumes to help students separate the learning. I use picture frames (frames of reference) when studying pollution. One group of students has a frame that says "politician," another group has a frame that says "new parent," another group has a frame that says "factory owner," and so on. Each group must talk about pollution according to the "frame of reference" they have been given. The frame serves as a *context* for the learning.

It is important to note here that Eric Jensen cites recent research in his workshops that provides evidence to support the fact that when we test students in the same room in which they learned the information, they do better on the test. In light of what we know about the episodic memory system, this makes sense.

THE PROCEDURAL MEMORY SYSTEM

Jensen (1997) says,

Procedural memory, also known as motor memory, includes that which happens when one, for example, learns to ride a bicycle, remembers the melody of a favorite song (musical memory), and recalls the fragrance of a flower (sensory memory). It is strongly brain compatible. Material learned this way is highly likely to be recalled; and in fact, this method is the most commonly used for early childhood learning. A child's life is full of actions, which require him or her to stand, ride, sit, try out, eat, move, play, build, or run. The learning is then embedded in the body; and therefore remembered.

Students from poverty have had many experiences learning this way. If they want to know how to do something, they generally learn by doing it. Adding movement to the learning is a great way to reach these students as well as ADD (attention-deficit disorder) and ADHD (attention-deficit/hyperactivity disorder) students. As a matter of fact, teachers trying to work with students from poverty or students with attention-deficit disorder or attention-deficit/hyperactivity disorder by teaching through lecture (semantic) are setting themselves and the students up for failure.

RETRIEVING FROM PROCEDURAL MEMORY

This system may be the strongest in terms of remembering. When we add movement to the learning, we tend to give it great strength in terms of storage and retrieval. Some teaching strategies that seem to reinforce this system include the following:

1. Role-playing

2. Drama

3. Choral reading

4. Projects

5. Hands-on activities

6. Manipulatives

7. Debates

8. Group activities

In my book *Ten Best Teaching Practices* (Tileston, 2000) and in the books by Marilee Sprenger (1999, 2002) you will find two other memory systems listed. Some researchers, such as Jensen (1997), say that while we first thought there were five memory systems, two of those systems are probably part of the original three. The two additional memory systems sometimes mentioned are:

Automatic memory: This is also found in the cerebellum and sometimes is called conditioned-response memory because the automaticity is a result of conditioning. Some examples of how this system is used include multiplication tables, the alphabet, and decoding skills. Using flashcards or songs in order to learn facts are ways of putting information into this system. Researchers such as Jensen (1997) believe that the automatic memory is really a part of the procedural memory system.

Emotional memory: Sprenger (2002) says, "This memory lane begins with the amygdala, the limbic structure that sifts through all incoming information for emotional content. The amygdala is very powerful and can take control of the brain." For this reason, attaching emotional memories to learning can make a tremendous difference in how material is remembered. The primary emotions are joy, fear, surprise, sadness, disgust, acceptance, anticipation, and anger. Using these will help reinforce learning. Some researchers believe that emotion is not a separate pathway but a factor that can enhance or shut down the other memory systems.

The truth is that there are probably memory systems that have not yet been discovered, but for now, the information about these three or five systems is important in helping all students to be successful.

Which of the three retrieval systems of the brain do you use most in your classroom? How can you use this information to strengthen your students' retrieval systems? Remember, you can combine retrieval systems to make them stronger. For example, adding movement (procedural) to learning facts (semantic) makes the stored information easier to retrieve.

5

Teaching for Declarative and Procedural Knowledge

I n the preceding chapters we have examined ways to help
students acquire and embed information and ways to help
them access that information when they need it. In this chapter
we will examine the two types of knowledge commonly used in
the classroom, and how we can use information about the brain
to help students to construct meaning and use the learning more
effectively.

Knowledge is usually categorized as declarative or procedural. Anytime students must perform a process, we think of
that knowledge as procedural. When we shoot baskets, write
a persuasive letter, read a bar graph, or set up an experiment,
we go through a series of steps that make up the process.

Information that requires component parts rather than a
series of steps is called declarative knowledge.

In putting together a lesson, the first step is to decide what
declarative knowledge needs to be taught and what procedural

knowledge needs to be taught. Since we learn each in a different way, it is important to distinguish between the two. We sometimes say that declarative knowledge is what we want students to "Know"; procedural knowledge is what we want students to be able to "Do."

DECLARATIVE KNOWLEDGE

Declarative knowledge refers to all of the things we want our students to know as a result of the lessons. For example, if I am teaching a unit on parts of speech, I will want my students to know the vocabulary associated with parts of speech, and I will want them to know the rules involved in using parts of speech in both written and spoken language. In order for my students to meet these goals, there are a series of processes that will take place in the brain. The following is a brief explanation of those processes.

CONSTRUCTING MEANING

We have discussed that it is essential for the brain to find meaning in the learning, otherwise the information is just a lot of incoming noise to be discarded. The following ideas are some of the ways that educators can help students construct meaning from the learning.

1. Create patterns and connections between what the learner already knows and the new learning. Our brain is a pattern-seeking device. Anytime new information comes into the brain, one of the first things the brain does is look for a pattern already present to which it can connect the new learning. If you have ever been in a situation where the speaker is talking about something for which you have no prior learning, you know that there is a moment of chaos and confusion while your brain searches for something to which to tie the new information. Many students without the prerequisite

skills to achieve go through this daily. For some the frustration does not end, because there is no prior knowledge with which to connect the learning. According to the meta-analysis by Marzano (1998), one of the most powerful ways that we can help our students is to provide a connection between the new learning and something they already know. This is much more than simply saying, "Last week we talked about . . ., this week we will talk about . . ." In the PBS series *Good Morning, Miss Toliver*, Kay Toliver relates fractions to pizza because pizzas are always sliced into fractional parts. She knows that her students love to eat and that they like pizza. It may have been a surprise to her inner-city students to learn that the fractional parts vary widely and that buying a slice of pizza for $2.00 is a bargain only if the fraction is large enough. Thus, the beginning of every lesson should involve helping students make connections between old knowledge and new knowledge. I may have students keep learning logs in which I ask them a question prior to the learning. For example, for a lesson on hunger, I might ask them to describe a time when they were really hungry. I might ask questions like, "What was your mood? Were you interested in anything but getting something to eat? Would this have been a good time for you to do your math?" In this case, I am building empathy because most of my students have not been really hungry in the way that starving populations experience. When studying an event in history, I might bring in pictures, music, smells, and tastes of the time.

2. Providing students with examples and non-examples is another way that we can build patterns in the learning. For instance, for a unit on symmetry, you may want to show students what is meant by symmetry by providing pictures and diagrams. Then you may want to show pictures and diagrams that do not have symmetry. Comparing and contrasting is another way to introduce a concept by showing examples and non-examples. You

might compare and contrast literary styles, points of view, mathematical concepts, or other concepts to show students the attributes of the subject you are discussing.

3. Organizing the information. The brain likes patterns, and anything we can do to help students organize declarative information will help them to understand and remember the learning. Remember that approximately 87% of learners either need to see the learning or do something with it. Using visuals with the learning will help students take in the information more efficiently, but even more important, it helps them to develop their own methods for organizing content. You might do this in several ways.

- Use pictographs
- Use charts and graphs
- Use graphic representations such as mind maps
- Provide note-taking models

STORING DECLARATIVE INFORMATION

Declarative (semantic) information must have a connector to help the brain remember it. Some connectors that you might use include:

- Provide visual representations when possible. These may be actual pictures or concrete objects, or they may be imaginary as you guide students through the thought processes to visualize what you are discussing. (It is important to note that students with limited English or students from poverty may not have the language to visualize what you are saying.)
- Use various mnemonic devices, such as H(uron), O(ntario), M(ichigan), E(rie), S(uperior) for the five Great Lakes.
- Color-code units or change the order of the classroom before a new unit.

PROCEDURAL KNOWLEDGE

Procedural knowledge refers to what we want our students to be able to do as a result of the learning. In a unit on parts of speech, I might want students to be able to use the parts of speech correctly in written and verbal language. I might assess their ability to do that by providing paragraphs with common errors for my students to identify and correct. There are several processes that procedural knowledge must pass through in order for the learning to become a part of long-term memory. These include the following:

CONSTRUCTING MENTAL MODELS

Just as the first phase of learning a skill or process is developing a rough model of the steps involved, so learning procedural knowledge is a matter of learning and understanding the steps involved in demonstrating the process. Some ways to do this include:

1. Teach students to talk through the process by demonstrating how you talk yourself through a process. For example, a French teacher might think aloud as she goes through the process of breaking a sentence into its grammatical parts.

2. Provide a written set of steps. For example, a teacher provides students with the written steps for writing a limerick and then demonstrates each step as she reads the limerick.

3. Provide models or examples for students.

4. Teach students to use flow charts or other visual models. For example, for a unit on weather, the teacher might have the students work in small groups to make a flow chart of the steps that take place in a weather pattern.

5. Teach students to mentally rehearse the steps involved in a process. For example, a physical education teacher might ask students to rehearse the process of shooting a basket before they actually try it with a basketball.

6. Connect the new skill to a skill they already know how to do.

SHAPING

Constructing an initial mental model for a new skill or process is just the first step in learning procedural knowledge. Once you actually begin to use the skill or process, you'll probably alter your initial model. You'll start to find out what works and what doesn't work and, in response, you'll modify your approach, adding some things and dropping others. This is called shaping. For example, after you constructed an initial model for performing long division, you began to discover some shortcuts and tricks that made the process work better for you (Marzano, 1992).

Some ways we can help students shape the procedural knowledge include:

1. Demonstrate and provide practice in the skill or process. As the teacher, it is important for you to provide general rules or heuristics in how to do a new process and then provide adequate opportunities for students to practice the learning before you assess.

2. Point out possible pitfalls or common errors that people make when executing the process. For example, a teacher showing students the steps involved in reading a contour map tells them that it is easy to misinterpret the altitudes for each contour layer and to make incorrect assumptions about specific types of contours.

3. Provide a variety of situations in which students can use a specific skill or process. For example, "a writing teacher demonstrates how she changes the decisions she makes during the editing process based on the audience for whom her writing is intended. She then has students edit a single essay for two different audiences and compare the results" (Marzano, 2001).

AUTOMATICITY

The last aspect of learning a new skill or process is doing something to the point where you can do it without conscious thought, or automaticity. Here are some guidelines to help you.

1. Provide adequate opportunities for practice. Help students self-assess the amount of practice they need and their speed and accuracy.

2. Have students keep a chart of their progress and to self-assess their work.

3. Provide opportunities for metacognition.

4. Give students a rubric with which they can self-assess their work. A rubric provides descriptors for each level of performance.

USING DECLARATIVE AND PROCEDURAL OBJECTIVES IN LESSONS

Let's look at these steps in regard to a lesson for elementary school and a lesson that might be used at the secondary level. For our elementary lesson, I will use the wonderful book by John Bianchi, *Snowed In at Pokeweed Public School.* For the secondary lesson, I will use one of my favorite O'Henry short stories, "After Twenty Years."

Elementary Sample Lesson

For the elementary lesson, I will set declarative goals for my students around what I want them to know from this lesson. For my lesson on *Snowed In at Pokeweed Public School*, my students will know:

1. The vocabulary from the book

2. The meaning of the concept of "snowed in"

3. The choices that the students made

4. The similarities and differences between the characters and themselves

5. The sequence of events

We know that there are some processes that the students must complete to meet these goals. The first process is to construct meaning from the story.

- How will I help my students construct meaning?

I will teach the vocabulary to my students by asking them first what they think the words mean and then by providing the definitions. I will ask the students to put the definitions in their own words.

I will use the tool "We'd Rather" to find out what kinds of choices my students would make if they were snowed in (see Figure 5.1). This also builds empathy for the characters in the story since I doubt that any of my students have been snowed in overnight at school. In this exercise, students put a circle around the things they would do if they were snowed in at school overnight.

We will have a class discussion about what the students do at Pokeweed that is like what we do at our school (e.g., ride a school bus, the teacher raising her hand when she wants the students to be quiet, have recess, play dodge ball, etc.). Then we will talk about how Pokeweed is different (the students are

Figure 5.1

For a lesson about *Snowed In at Pokeweed Public School* by John Bianchi

If you were snowed in at school, which of the following would you do?

animals, they eat hayburgers instead of hamburgers, their teacher is a cow).

In small groups, students will discuss the sequence of events.

- How will I help my students organize the information?

Students will use drawings to decide what choices they would make if snowed in.

I will show pictures from the book on the overhead or LCD projection device. (Current copyright law allows you to make copies of some of the pictures from the book to show the students for educational purposes. Check with your librarian for the law in your state.)

Students will use a chart to compare and contrast (see Form 5.1).

Form 5.1   Compare/Contrast

Compare/Contrast

Pokeweed   My School

How Are They Alike?

. . . .

. . . .

. . . .

. . . .

. . . .

. . . .

. . . .

. . . .

How Are They Different in Regard to:
Eating

Students

Activities

Weather

- How will I help my students store the information?

  I will help to build relevance by asking students what they would do if snowed in.
  1. I will use visuals to help give the learning a connection.
  2. I will use advance organizers such as the compare and contrast chart to help students put the information into a pattern.
  3. Students will draw pictures of their definitions of the vocabulary words.

The procedural objectives indicate what I want my students to be able to do as a result of the learning. The procedural objectives for this lesson might be written like this:
Students will be able to:

1. Compare and contrast the characters from the book with their own classroom using a compare/contrast chart.

2. Sequence the events from the story using pictures and words.

To assure myself that my students will be able to meet the objectives, I will include a series of processes. The first of those is to help students create mental models of the learning.

- How will I help my students construct mental models?

  I will provide examples of how to complete a compare-and-contrast chart.
  1. I will provide feedback as my students construct their models.
  2. I will provide sample pictures for my students and provide feedback as my students work.
  3. I will provide the pictures for the sequence-of-events chart and offer advice and encouragement as my students work.

- How will I provide shaping for my students?

  I will provide a nonthreatening atmosphere for my students to construct their models by making it OK to make mistakes as long as they are corrected along the way.

1. I will provide frequent and specific feedback to my students as they work.
2. I will provide an opportunity for students to work with others so that they get feedback from their peers.
3. I will allow students to start over when needed.
4. I will provide adequate time for practice.
5. Students will self-evaluate their compare/contrast models using a rubric describing levels of performance and will complete a group evaluation of their sequencing model with an accompanying rubric.

- How will I help my students gain automaticity?

Students will be asked to think about the learning and to provide feedback using the models provided.

Now, let's look at how this might be accomplished in a secondary classroom.

Secondary Sample Lesson

- Secondary lesson on "After Twenty Years."

For my declarative objectives, I will examine what I want students to know as a result of their study of this short story (see Form 5.2).

For the secondary lesson, I will set goals for my students around what I want them to know from this lesson. They might be written like this.

Students will know:

1. The vocabulary from the story

2. The choices that the two characters must make

3. The reasons for the choices

4. That we all make difficult choices with which we must live

■ How will I help my students construct meaning?

I will teach the vocabulary to my students through questioning strategies.

1. I will use the tool "We'd Rather" to find out what kinds of choices my students would make if they were in the position of the main character. This also builds empathy for the characters in the story.

Next, we will use a debate format to discuss the choices of the characters and what makes a "good friend."

Last, students will identify how far they think someone should go to fulfill a job responsibility.

■ How will I help my students organize the information?

1. Students will identify the vocabulary words they know, the ones they have heard but whose definition they are not sure of, and the ones they do not know at all (see Form 5.3).
2. Students will read a small portion of the story and then, using the Prediction Tree tool, will decide what will happen next. For a Prediction Tree exercise, students read a paragraph or group of paragraphs. Based on that information, they make a prediction

Form 5.2   "After Twenty Years." by O'Henry

Would Do	Would Not Do
1. Pretend to be someone else	
2. Send someone else to do my "dirty work"	
3. Betray a friend	
4. Do my job no matter what the cost	

Form 5.3   Teaching Vocabulary

Vocabulary Word	Definition	Have Heard the Word Before	Never Heard the Word Before	Know the Definition
1.				
2.				
3.				

about what is going to happen in the story. They must support their predictions (see Form 5.4)—for example, I might ask, "What was said, done, thought that made you think this would happen?" This is also a good tool to practice extrapolating data and the difference between fact and opinion.

3. Students will complete a continuum on what they would do to fulfill a job responsibility.

- How will I help my students store the information?

    1. I will help to build relevance by asking students what they would do if they had to make the same choice as the main character.
    2. I will use advance organizers like the Prediction Tree chart to help students put the information into a pattern.

Form 5.4   The Prediction Tree

Proof	Prediction	Proof

Proof	Prediction	Proof

Proof	Prediction	Proof

Proof	Prediction	Proof

S
U
B
J
E
C
T

3. Students will chart their understanding of the definitions of the vocabulary words.

My objectives for procedural knowledge might look something like this:
Students will be able to:

1. Identify and chart vocabulary words using the chart given.

2. Chart on a continuum how they would make the decision made by the main character.

3. Predict the conclusion of the story using the Prediction Tree.

- How will I help my students construct models?

    1. I will provide examples of how to complete the various charts.
    2. I will provide guided practice as my students create their models.
    3. I will provide ample time for discussion and for creating the models.
    4. I will provide the materials needed for the models.

- How will I provide shaping for my students?

    1. I will provide a nonthreatening atmosphere for my students to construct their models by making it OK to make mistakes as long as they are corrected along the way.
    2. I will provide frequent feedback to my students as they work.
    3. I will provide an opportunity for students to work with others so that they are provided feedback from their peers.
    4. I will allow students to start over when needed.
    5. I will provide adequate time for practice.
    6. Students will self-evaluate their Prediction Tree models.

- How will I help my students internalize the information?

    1. We will begin with an exercise to connect the new learning to things they already know, such as holding down a job, being a friend, and so on.
    2. We will write in our Learning Logs about individual responses to the story.

6

Building a Model to Facilitate Learning

In the preceding chapters we talked about those factors that make us smart—the ability to take in information quickly and efficiently and the ability to retrieve information when it is needed. While we cannot control all of the processes involved, there are certain processes that the classroom teacher can facilitate to help ensure that students will be able to learn at a more efficient rate and that they will gain better access to their memory pathways.

A step-by-step model follows that may help as you plan for your own students.

In summary: Through current research we can, for the first time in history, work smarter, not just harder. Scientists have only begun to open the doors to the way our brain learns and remembers. That the research is so involved and difficult to obtain is a testimony to the fact that our brain is a complicated and wonderful mechanism. We do, however, have at our

Form 6.1   Step-by-Step Model to Facilitate Student Learning

Step One: Planning for the learning using declarative and procedural objectives.

Choose a lesson that you will soon teach in your own classroom. For that lesson answer the following questions using the information from this book.

What are your objectives for the lesson?

Declarative Objectives: Students will know:

1.

2.

3.

Procedural Objectives: Students will be able to:

1.

2.

3.

Step Two: How will you use the senses to introduce the learning?

Visual:

Auditory:

Olfactory:

Touch:

Taste:

(Continued)

Form 6.1 Continued

Step Three: To which modalities are you teaching? How are you doing this?

Visual:

Auditory:

Kinesthetic:

Step Four: Information processing

What will you do to ensure that students link new knowledge to old knowledge?

Generate an internal representation of the new knowledge through graphic organizers?

Step Five: Working memory

How will you ensure that students make better use of the memory lanes, specifically:

Semantic memory:

Episodic memory:

Procedural memory:

Step Six: Assessment

How will you communicate your learning expectations to your students?

disposal information to help more students be successful in the classroom. We also have information to help us make more informed decisions about how to teach students. In the past, our decisions about how to teach were often made on the basis of trial and error, but now we have specific data to help us make good choices. For example, we know that slow learners need the learning to be reinforced in their preferred modality. We also know that most of our students need to "see" the learning before it makes sense to them. We know that linguistic and nonlinguistic models are brain friendly, because the brain likes connections and because most students are visual learners. Before our students send information to long-term storage, the learning must not only make sense but also have personal meaning for them. This is very different from previous models that emphasized that learning needs to make sense but said very little about the need for personal meaning.

We really do live in an exciting time for education. In spite of the tremendous pressure on teachers to teach to all students and to make sure students are ready for testing, we have more information available to us than ever before about how to make students successful.

Vocabulary Summary

Achievement Gap

The word *achievement* means level of attainment or proficiency. If there is a gap in that level of attainment, analyze the data to find out why a certain group or groups are not attaining at the rate of the general group.

For example, as you look at test data on your students, look at how much gain the regular education students are making yearly. Let's say that your regular education group is making a 1.2 gain, or 1 year 2 months. Now look to see whether the same gain is being made by Title One students, gifted students, males, females, Hispanics, African Americans, Native Americans, and others. If not, there is an achievement gap for those students.

Active Learning

Active learning involves information processing and knowledge utilization by the brain. Examples are decision making, inquiry, investigation, problem solving, compare/contrast, and more. Instruction that encompasses information processing and knowledge utilization involves the use of heuristics—general rules for learning procedural knowledge.

Basic Skills

Basic skills are foundation knowledge and skills students are expected to acquire in elementary and middle school in such areas as reading, writing, and mathematics.

The Association for Supervisors and Curriculum Developers (ASCD) provides the following definition: "The fundamental skills needed to succeed in school and eventually in life. Most people think of basic skills as the ability to read, write, and compute. Others, however, would broaden the term to include such skills as the ability to use a computer, the ability to work cooperatively with others, or even the temperament to cope with continuous change."

Brain-Based Teaching

This is teaching using the tools that have been determined to be brain compatible. For example, teachers who teach to the three modalities of learning or who provide ways for students to activate the brain pathways are using brain-based teaching.

Coaching

Educators use the term *coaching* to refer to any situation in which someone helps someone else learn a skill. The teacher may be the coach, but students may also act as coaches.

Cognitive Development

Cognitive development begins at birth. It is the process of learning through sensory perception, memory, and observation. Children are born into cultures and backgrounds that affect what they learn as well as how they learn. Children from enriched environments (in which parents and caregivers read to and with them, teach them letters and numbers, and take them to plays and museums) come to school prepared to learn. Children from impoverished or abusive backgrounds often lack most or all of these preschool advantages. To stimulate the cognitive development of these children, teachers use strategies such as placing learning into general information with specific learning situations.

Constructivism

Constructivism is an approach to teaching based on research about how people learn. Many researchers say that each individual "constructs" meaning rather than receiving it from others. People disagree about how to achieve constructive learning, but many educators believe that students come to understand abstract concepts best through exploration, reasoning, and discussion.

Constructivism uses brain research on meaning making by first connecting new learning to what the student already knows or has experienced. Next, constructivism helps students to create patterns to help the brain store information more effectively and to help students retrieve information when needed. Constructivism shows teachers how to make better use of all of the brain's pathways, not just the semantic.

Declarative Knowledge

Declarative knowledge answers the "what" of learning. It answers what something is, what it means, and what is to be learned. Declarative knowledge might include steps, facts, concepts, understandings, and generalizations. We assess declarative knowledge by asking students to give examples and attributes, and to identify how things are alike and different. Much of what we test in school is declarative knowledge; for example, students cannot describe a fraction if they do not know what it is and how it is used. Declarative knowledge comes before procedural knowledge, which involves skills and processes.

Differentiated Instruction

Differentiated instruction provides for a range of student differences in the same classroom by using different learning materials, assigning different tasks, and using other practices, such as cooperative learning.

Teachers who demonstrate differentiated instruction accept and build upon the premise that learners differ in important ways (Tomlinson, 1999). They provide specific ways for each individual to learn well, without deviating from high standards. The teacher makes consistent efforts to respond to learners' needs, guided by general principles of classroom facilitation, which effectively attend to individuals. Content, process, and product are systematically modified based on student readiness. Key principles of a differentiated classroom include the following:

- The teacher is clear about what is important in the lesson.
- The teacher understands, appreciates, and builds upon student differences.
- Instruction and assessment work together.
- The teacher monitors and adjusts content, process, and results.
- Individual success and maximum growth are the two main goals.
- Flexibility is necessary for implementation of differentiation.

Differentiated instruction involves modification for three key reasons (Tomlinson, 1999): access to learning, motivation to learn, and efficiency of learning. All of these areas can be linked to student readiness, interest, and learning.

Episodic Memory

The *episodic memory* system has to do with context. Where were you when you learned the information and in what context did you learn it? This is a strong memory system, especially when details are revisited from time to time. This is the memory system that allows us to remember where we were when some event in history took place even though the event may have happened many years ago. The details tend to get distorted over time, but the general information remains within the memory system. Add emotion to this memory system, and the length of time we can remember is almost limitless. We can activate this memory system by field trips, putting information up visually in the room, creating simulations, color-coding the units or the vocabulary sheets, and testing students in the same room in which they learned the information. We always do better math in the math classroom than we do in the English classroom. It has to do with this memory system, which is most comfortable where it first learned the information. What are the implications for testing students in a cafeteria?

Teachers who teach the material should also be the ones who test it with students, especially when using high-stakes tests. Substitute teachers get poorer results from students in an assessment situation because of the episodic memory system.

Explicit Instruction

Explicit instruction is a teacher-directed strategy that includes such methods as lecture, didactic questioning, drill and practice, and/or demonstrations to teach specific skill information or the steps involved in a process. For example, with explicit instruction that introduces and applies nonlinguistic organizers, students are better able to facilitate their use. The steps involved in explicit instruction include controlled examples and practice guided by the teacher, including examples and non-examples.

Next, students are involved in guided practice in which they practice the learning with the teacher present to give immediate feedback.

Third, students are moved to independent practice where they practice the learning without the teacher present as they work (e.g., homework).

Graphic Organizers

Graphic organizers make a great teaching strategy to help students create a mental picture of semantic information to embed or store in long-term memory for later access or retrieval. The brain stores and retrieves pictures more easily than words. Graphic organizers help students to use "deep processing" to embed the learning into the brain. Graphic organizers are visual organizers that help organize information into a pattern to link new knowledge to prior knowledge.

Making mental pictures, drawing pictures, and engaging students in kinesthetic activity can be successfully used in graphic organizers.

Heuristics

Heuristics are the general rules, tactics, and strategies, as opposed to a set of rigid steps, for implementing processes such as decision making, experimental inquiry, problem solving, investigation, reading, speaking, and listening. Students apply and practice the general rules, tactics, and strategies with attention to how they might be improved. When teachers provide students with a guide that outlines the components and subcomponents of a process, they are providing students with a heuristic. For the purpose of this book, a heuristic is defined as a loosely organized set of skills, tactics or strategies represented verbally, linguistically, or graphically, and used as a guide to facilitate the performance of an overall process such as writing, speaking, reading, listening, problem solving, decision making, inquiry, and investigation.

Indirect Instruction

Indirect instruction is instruction that is centered on activities by the students. Students learn by discovery, by creating, and by finding information on the topic rather than being instructed directly by the teacher.

Mastery Learning

A way of organizing instruction that tries to ensure that students have mastered (learned material at the 80% level or better) each increment of a subject before going on to the next. The idea assumes that a subject can be subdivided into sequential steps organized hierarchically. The classic *mastery learning* model formulated by psychologist Benjamin Bloom calls for teachers to teach a unit of work and give a formative test. Students who do not master the material study it in a different way, while the mastery students do enrichment work. Then all students take a summative test, which nearly all students are expected to pass.

Metacognition

Metacognition is the process of thinking about thinking. When teachers provide classroom opportunities for students to reflect on the learning and to make judgments about the learning, students are more likely to remember the learning. (Teachers are helping to give the learning meaning for the students.) Some ways that teachers can do this include:

- **Journaling:** Students write to a specific prompt about the learning. It may be as explicit as, "Name one thing that you do not understand about the learning," or general as, "Write your perceptions about the causes of the conflict in the story."

Journaling has a strong impact on student learning.

- **Ticket Out The Door:** Students must write on a sheet of paper one thing they learned today and one thing they still do not understand. This is their ticket out the door at the end of the class or day. Many variations of this are possible, such as asking students to show one way they might use their math lesson or a word or phrase that they might use (in French) if visiting a museum in France.
- **What, So What, Now What:** Students fill out the questions with *What* they have learned, *So What* does it have to do with them, and *Now What* is one way they can use the information in the real world.
- **PMI:** *P* is for positive, as in name three things that you learned today or liked about the lesson today; *M* is for

minus, as in what are some things that are bothering you about the lesson or what are you still confused about; and *I* is for interesting, as in do you have an interesting observation, question, or idea that you want to add to the lesson.

Pedagogy

Pedagogy is the art and science of teaching—especially the conscious use of particular instructional methods. When teachers use a discovery approach rather than direct instruction, for example, they are using a different pedagogy.

> The National Academy Press released the results of an intensive two-year survey of the scientific research on learning and concluded . . . both subject-matter knowledge and pedagogical knowledge are important for expert teaching. The study documented that teachers need a solid knowledge of how the cultural beliefs and personal characteristics of learners influence the learning process. . . . Studies of teaching conclude that expertise consists of more than a set of general methods that can be applied across all subject matter. . . . Teachers need to acquire an understanding of effective teaching methods for each of the subject areas that they teach. (Gene Carter, Executive Director, *ASCD*, June 13, 2002)

Procedural Knowledge

Procedural knowledge involves skills and processes. Where declarative knowledge involves "What students know," procedural knowledge is involved with "What students are able to do." Declarative knowledge usually precedes procedural knowledge.

Procedural knowledge is often equated with assessments that require students to demonstrate their knowledge of a given topic. Rubrics may be used to determine the level of success for procedural knowledge. Examples of procedural knowledge include editing written compositions for spelling, grammar, and mechanics; reading for comprehension (macro process); and performing mathematical tasks.

Procedural Memory

Procedural memory is stored in the cerebellum, which is responsible for muscle coordination. Processes such as driving a car are stored in this part of the brain. This memory system has to do with activities that involve the body. Unlike semantic memory, procedural memory is enhanced by rote rehearsal. We use this memory system a great deal in early childhood but less and less each year in school as the years progress (except in vocational classes, physical education, and fine arts). This is a strong memory system and can enhance the semantic system if the two are used together. Adding movement and hands-on activities are ways to activate this memory system in the classroom.

Scaffolding

The way a teacher provides support to make sure students succeed at complex tasks they couldn't do otherwise is called *scaffolding*. Most teaching is done as the students go about the task, rather than before they start. For example, as a group of elementary students proceeds to publish a student newspaper, the teacher shows them how to conduct interviews, write news stories, and prepare captions for photographs. Because the teacher supports the students to make sure they don't fail in their effort, it reminds researchers of the scaffolding that workers sometimes place around buildings. As the students become more skillful, the teacher gives them more responsibility, taking away the scaffolding when it is no longer needed. This gradual withdrawal has been called fading.

Scaffolding can be used with whole groups, small groups, or individual instruction, although it is challenging to reach all students successfully in a large group setting. Smaller groups provide opportunities for teachers to encourage each child to participate in the activity and allow teachers to supply the strategy or information individual students need to become successful. Sensitive scaffolding of a student's learning is based on knowing what the student has already learned, what the student is capable of learning with assistance, and what is currently beyond that student's grasp. Most students benefit from some level of teacher assistance. The teacher provides whatever is needed to help the student be successful, gradually contributing less support as the student assumes more of the process independently. The teacher's ultimate goal is to become less and less involved as the student eventually becomes an independent learner. Teachers can help students self-regulate through the processes of routines and self-monitoring.

Routines: A routine is a sequence of steps that becomes automatic through repetition. Initially, the teacher provides the structure for approaching (for example) a literacy task, repeating the same sequence over the course of the school year, often using the same language. This systematic talk is a way of sharing thinking with the student. By thinking aloud, the teacher demonstrates how to work through different tasks. Gradually the student adopts the routine, and the guidance process becomes less explicit, moving the student toward student independence.

Self-Monitoring: When students are able to share their thinking by telling how they went about attacking and accomplishing a task, they are at a level of awareness called self-monitoring. By asking individual students to share their thinking, the teacher can monitor student thought processes and demonstrate what they should be doing for themselves. When students have taken over the job of self-monitoring by continually asking themselves if what they are reading or writing makes sense, without prompts from the teacher, they have reached the final step of successful self-monitoring.

Semantic Memory

Semantic memory holds the information that we learn from words or facts. It is the memory system most used in school and the least efficient of the memory systems. In order to remember the information, there must be a hook or connection. The brain is not very good at remembering meaningless facts. There are three basic learning hooks that help students not only learn but remember. The first hook is relevance. We learn information better when we see the relevance in the learning. Tell students up front why they are learning the information and how they will use it in the real world. The more you can connect the information to their immediate world, the more likely they will pay attention to the information. In a workshop that I attended, William Glasser said he could teach anyone anything as long as he could give it relevance. He said that, after all, young children have learned one of the hardest things to learn; they have learned a language and no one had to stand in front of them with flashcards. They learned it because it was relevant to their world.

The second hook is pattern. The brain likes patterns, and when it receives new information, the first thing that it seems to do is look for what it already knows or has experienced as a hook for the new learning. When possible, create a connection or pattern at the beginning of a lesson to help students hook the new information.

The third hook is emotion. Add a little emotion to your classroom through music, simulations, visuals, drama, and debates. Emotion is the strongest force in the brain; it has the power to shut down our thinking or to enhance it.

Teaching for Understanding

Engaging students in learning activities intended to help them understand the complexities of a topic is referred to as teaching for understanding. *Teaching for understanding* is different from teaching simply for recall, which results in students being able to answer questions without knowing what their answers really mean. Specialists advise that a good way to know whether students understand is to ask them to perform a task that demonstrates they can apply and make use of what they have learned in a realistic setting. For example, students might participate in a mock trial to demonstrate that they have developed their understanding of the rights of the accused.

By nature, teaching for understanding is procedural; that is, it involves "What can students do with the information?"

Teaching for understanding usually involves higher-level thinking skills such as analysis (breaking down information into manageable parts), synthesis (breaking something down and then putting it back together in new and unusual ways), and evaluation (making a judgment about something).

Vocabulary
Post-Test

At the beginning of this book, you were given a vocabulary list and a pre-test on that vocabulary. Below are the post-test and the answer key for the vocabulary assessment.

VOCABULARY POST-TEST

Instructions: Choose the one best answer for each question.

1. Which of the following is *not* true of teaching for understanding?
   A. It is procedural in nature.
   B. It involves being able to repeat declarative information.
   C. It encourages higher-level thinking.
   D. It requires demonstration of understanding.

2. Which of the following is *not* a declarative objective?
   A. Students will learn vocabulary words.
   B. Students will understand the meaning of semantic memory.
   C. Students will develop a model for understanding semantic memory.
   D. Students will understand the importance of semantic memory.

3. Which of the following is an example of chunking?
   A. Read pages 17-22 in the text.
   B. Answer Questions 4-20 on the worksheet.
   C. Place your ideas for why we have world hunger in the categories provided.
   D. Choose the topic you would like to use for your project.

4. Which of the following is true of semantic memory?
   A. It is brain-compatible.
   B. It requires a great deal of intrinsic motivation.
   C. Its capacity is limitless.
   D. It is contextual in nature.

5. What is an example of procedural memory?
   A. Memorizing vocabulary
   B. Listening to lecture
   C. Watching television
   D. Driving a car

6. Which of the following is an example of episodic memory?
   A. Listening to lecture
   B. Going on a field trip
   C. Driving a car
   D. Memorizing vocabulary

7. Which of the following is an example of indirect instruction?
   A. The teacher takes the students to the library so they can do research on a given topic.
   B. The teacher introduces and explains the vocabulary words.
   C. The teacher reads a story to the children, stopping to ask questions.
   D. The teacher provides an outline on the board of the skeletal system.

8. A teacher usually uses scaffolding . . .
   A. At the conclusion of a unit
   B. At the beginning point in learning a process

    C. With gifted students

    D. With visual learners

9. Which of the following is an example of scaffolding?

    A. Students look up the definitions to their vocabulary words.

    B. Students work in small groups to define their vocabulary words.

    C. The teacher leads students in a discussion of the vocabulary words then asks them to provide their own definitions for the words.

    D. The teacher places students in small groups and asks them to brainstorm uses of their vocabulary words.

10. When would coaching most likely *not* be used?

    A. When students are working in cooperative learning groups.

    B. When students are doing seatwork.

    C. When the teacher is lecturing.

    D. When the teacher is using a questioning technique.

11. Which of the following is an example of a declarative objective?

    A. Students will provide examples of nonlinguistic organizers.

    B. Students will develop sentences using the vocabulary provided.

    C. Students will compare and contrast parts of speech.

    D. Students will know the steps used in writing a paper.

12. Metacognition (which is *not* true) . . .

    A. Helps the brain remember the learning.

    B. Should be a part of every lesson.

    C. Can be processed through a PMI.

    D. Is a step in mastery learning.

13. Declarative objectives . . .

    A. Require the development of a model

    B. Require knowledge and comprehension

C. Require movement

D. Require chunking

14. Authentic learning . . .
    A. Requires rote rehearsal
    B. Requires extrinsic rewards
    C. Requires memorization
    D. Requires active brain processing

15. Which is *not* an example of explicit instruction?
    A. Cooperative learning
    B. Questioning
    C. Lecture
    D. Demonstrations

16. Procedural objectives . . .
    A. Tell the "what" of the learning
    B. Use primarily the semantic memory system
    C. Involve the facts and vocabulary to memorize
    D. Involve action on the part of the learner

17. Teaching for understanding . . .
    A. Usually involves simple recall
    B. Usually involves higher-level thinking
    C. Usually involves only declarative objectives
    D. Usually involves primarily at-risk students

18. Organizers . . .
    A. Are all nonlinguistic
    B. Are a tool for auditory learners
    C. Are a part of meaning making
    D. Are sequential

19. Which is *not* an example of pedagogy?
    A. Teaching a lesson
    B. Planning a lesson
    C. Applying for a teaching job
    D. Assessing students

20. Which of the following is *not* true of metacognition?
    A. Metacognition is an activity designed to be used
       throughout a lesson.

B. Metacognition can be teacher directed.
C. Metacognition should be a part of all lessons.
D. Metacognition has a low impact on student success.

VOCABULARY POST-TEST ANSWER KEY

1. A	11. D
2. C	12. D
3. C	13. B
4. B	14. D
5. D	15. A
6. B	16. D
7. A	17. B
8. B	18. C
9. C	19. C
10. C	20. D

References

Anderson, J. R. (1995). *Learning and memory: An integrated approach.* New York: John Wiley.

Gazzaniga, M. (1992). *Nature's mind.* New York: Basic Books.

Jensen, E. (1997). *Completing the puzzle: The brain-compatible approach to learning.* Del Mar, CA: The Brain Store.

Marzano, R. (1998). *A theory-based meta-analysis of research on instruction.* Aurora, CO: Mid-continent Regional Educational Laboratory.

Marzano, R. J. (1992). *A different kind of classroom: Teaching with dimensions of learning.* Alexandria, VA: Association for Supervision and Curriculum Development.

Marzano, R. J. (2001). *Designing a new taxonomy of educational objectives.* Thousand Oaks, CA: Corwin Press.

Marzano, R. J., Pickering, D. J., & Pollock, J. E. (2001). *Classroom instruction that works.* Alexandria, VA: Association for Supervision and Curriculum Development.

Payne, R. K. (2001). *A framework for understanding poverty.* Highlands, TX: Aha! Process Inc.

Sousa, D. (1995). *How the brain learns.* Reston, VA: National Association of Secondary School Principals.

Sousa, D. (2001). How the brain learns (2nd ed.). Thousand Oakss, CA: Corwin Press.

Sprenger, M. (1999). *Learning and memory: The brain in action.* Alexandria, VA: Association for Supervision and Curriculum Development.

Sprenger, M. (2002). *Becoming a wiz at brain-based teaching: How to make every year your best year.* Thousand Oaks, CA: Corwin Press.

Tileston, D. W. (2000). *Ten best teaching practices: How brain research, learning styles, and standards define teaching competencies.* Thousand Oaks, CA: Corwin Press.

Tomlinson, C. A. (1999). *The differentiated classroom: Responding to the needs of all learners.* Alexandria, VA: Association of Supervisors and Curriculum Developers (ASCD).

Index

**CORWIN
PRESS**

The Corwin Press logo—a raven striding across an open book—represents the happy union of courage and learning. We are a professional-level publisher of books and journals for K-12 educators, and we are committed to creating and providing resources that embody these qualities. Corwin's motto is "Success for All Learners."